Original title:
After We Broke

Author: Aron Pilviste
ISBN HARDBACK: 978-9916-89-811-6
ISBN PAPERBACK: 978-9916-89-812-3
ISBN EBOOK: 978-9916-89-813-0

Whispers of the Shattered Soul

In the quiet, shadows play,
Hearts once bright now drift away.
Whispers touch the hollowed night,
Seeking solace, searching light.

In broken shards, our spirits sigh,
Yearning for the reasons why.
Hope, a flicker in despair,
Dancing softly in the air.

Echoes of the past resound,
Truth in silence can be found.
With every tear that falls like rain,
We find strength in our shared pain.

In the stillness, faith can mend,
A gentle heart will always tend.
To heal the wounds that once felt cold,
A love transcending, pure and bold.

So let us kneel, our spirits blend,
In whispered prayers, to the end.
The shattered soul will rise again,
With faith that conquers every sin.

Echoes of Lost Devotion

In the remnants, echoes call,
Fading whispers through the hall.
Once a heart so full of grace,
Now just shadows, lost in space.

Promises made, now turned to dust,
In the void, we place our trust.
Searching for the warmth we knew,
In the silence, longing's true.

Time has turned the page of fate,
In stillness, love can never wait.
Yet within the aching chest,
Lies a hope that won't unrest.

With every prayer, we stitch the seams,
Dreaming still of radiant beams.
Though devotion may seem far,
In our hearts, it's where we are.

So let the echoes softly play,
Guiding us through night and day.
In every stumble, every fall,
We'll rise again, through it all.

Sanctity in Fractured Faith

In the struggle, we find light,
Through the darkness, find our sight.
Fractured dreams, yet still we rise,
With open hearts, we touch the skies.

Sanctity in every scar,
Guiding us, no matter how far.
Faith is whispered through the pain,
In every tear, there's strength to gain.

Listen close, the spirit speaks,
In the silence, hope it seeks.
Finding beauty in the broken,
In the shambles, love's unspoken.

Let the faith within us grow,
With every challenge, spirit flows.
Trust the journey, hold it tight,
In the shadows, seek the light.

Though fractured, we are not alone,
In every heart, a sacred home.
Together, in this sacred way,
We'll find our peace at end of day.

The Altar of Forgotten Promises

In humble space, we gather round,
Where whispers of our hopes abound.
Promises made with pure intent,
Now linger on, like echoes spent.

The altar stands, time worn and aged,
With stories of the hearts engaged.
Forgotten vows in twilight gleam,
In silence, we ignite the dream.

Hands once held, now drift apart,
Yet love remains, a sacred art.
In every promise, lost or found,
Resides a truth that knows no bound.

We gather here in faith renewed,
In whispers, love's eternal food.
Against the tides of loss and pain,
We'll sing our song, and rise again.

So let us kneel, and mend the fray,
The altar calls, we must obey.
In every tear, a seed is sown,
For in our hearts, we'll find our home.

The Wayfarer's Prayer for You

Dear wanderer, find your light,
In shadows cast by night.
May grace guide every step,
In whispers softly kept.

Hold faith close to your heart,
In trials, never part.
When burdens weigh you down,
Look up to wear your crown.

Through valleys dark and deep,
Let hope within you leap.
For every tear you shed,
May peace pour in instead.

In the quiet, seek the place,
Where love grants warm embrace.
Trust in sacred hands above,
To light your path with love.

As you journey on your way,
Feel strength in each new day.
For in this prayer, you'll find,
A spirit intertwined.

Candelabra of Broken Dreams

In the dark, a flicker glows,
Hope ignites where sorrow flows.
These dreams once bright, now dimmed,
In shadows, softly rimmed.

Each candle holds a whisper,
Of a wish, a silent lister.
Though flames may dance and sway,
Their light shall not decay.

For every broken heart's plea,
Is a seed for destiny.
In fragments, beauty shines,
Through paths divine, it aligns.

Let each candelabra shine,
With faith, resolve, entwine.
For in the night's embrace,
New dreams find their rightful place.

As shadows stretch and bend,
Remember love won't end.
In time, through pain and strife,
A brighter dream springs to life.

Intercessions of Lost Affection

In the hush where echoes lie,
Softly spoken, a gentle sigh.
For every love that's flown,
A prayer for seeds we've sown.

In whispers of the heart's refrain,
We gather strength from our pain.
Though distance holds us tight,
The soul connects in light.

For moments lost to time's embrace,
We seek the warmth of grace.
In every tear we shed,
A testament of love, still spread.

By intercessions deep and true,
We mend the broken view.
In every prayer, a spark,
To reignite love's arc.

As we journey through the night,
With hope as our guiding light,
For every lost affection dear,
A sacred bond draws near.

Chronicles of Celestial Parting

Beneath the stars, we part ways,
In silence deep, our hearts blaze.
Each memory, a sacred thread,
Weaving stories long since said.

In celestial hands, we trust,
To guide us back, as we must.
With every breath, a prayer sent,
For love, though far, is not spent.

The universe holds our song,
In harmony, we belong.
Though earthly ties may fray,
In spirit, we shall stay.

As paths diverge under night's dome,
Remember, you're never alone.
For every star whispers light,
Binding souls in cosmic flight.

When time brings us back around,
In joy, we shall be found.
For in our hearts, we chart,
The chronicles, never apart.

Prayers Beneath the Shattered Sky

In the silence, I cry out,
Whispers of hope, soft and bright.
The heavens weep with sorrow,
Yet my heart still seeks the light.

Each tear a prayer, each sigh,
Echoes of faith in despair.
Beneath this shattered sky, I fly,
For divine grace will always care.

Lost in shadows, I wander,
Seeking the path of peace.
A promise held in wonder,
In stillness, my soul finds release.

Heaven's gaze upon my face,
Guiding me through the night.
In the dark, I find my place,
In the ashes, sparks ignite.

So I pray, with broken voice,
For love to mend what's torn.
In this journey, I rejoice,
For rebirth comes from the worn.

Divine Echoes of What Was

In the echoes of the past,
I hear the whispers in the wind.
Fading memories hold me fast,
A light where shadows had been.

The heavens sing a low refrain,
Of love that traveled through the years.
In anguish, joy, and even pain,
The music weaves through all my tears.

Each moment holds a sacred space,
In the tapestry of grace divine.
Weaving time, it leaves a trace,
A reminder of the sacred line.

As I tread on holy ground,
I seek the blessings yet to come.
In silence, holy truths abound,
In the stillness, hearts can hum.

So let the echoes guide my heart,
In every prayer, in every sigh.
For from the end, new hopes impart,
Divine reflections in the sky.

The Pilgrimage of Forgotten Love

In the valley, where silence reigns,
I wander with memories close.
Each footstep carries gentle pains,
Yet love's warmth is what I chose.

Through fields of green and skies of gray,
I search for remnants of the past.
In every heartbeat, come what may,
The shadows seek a love to cast.

With faith, I climb the steep ascent,
Within my soul, a fire burns.
Each moment, every time well spent,
In these pages, the spirit learns.

The journey teaches heart to mend,
And every prayer unfolds a plan.
Through trials, love transcends the end,
In sacred bonds, a holy span.

So on this path, my heart will soar,
A pilgrimage eternally.
For love, forgotten, yearns for more,
In every breath, divinity.

Beneath the Ruins of Us

In the ruins where we built our dreams,
Echoes linger like fading light.
Fragments of love in silent screams,
Yet hope finds a way to ignite.

Through the ashes of what we knew,
Life's lessons carved in tender stone.
In every heartbeat, shadows grew,
But in loss, I've never been alone.

We forged our paths in endless night,
With faith as our guiding star.
In the darkness, we searched for light,
Though lost, we wandered far.

Among the ruins, I seek your face,
The memory lingers like a prayer.
In the stillness, I feel your grace,
For love's spirit is always there.

So I gather the pieces, hold them tight,
In this sacred space, love's embrace.
Beneath the ruins, shining bright,
Hearts will heal, and find their place.

Atonement of the Faded

In shadows deep, where sins reside,
The light of grace does softly guide.
With whispered prayers, the heart lays bare,
Forgiveness sought in tender care.

The weight of sorrow, heavy laid,
Yet hope's renewal breaks the shade.
In silent cries, the spirit bends,
To seek the peace that mercy sends.

Within the dawn, redemption shines,
As faith in love, the soul entwines.
With every tear, the past we mend,
And find the strength to rise again.

Through trials faced, we walk as one,
In unity, our battles won.
A tapestry of grace we weave,
In holy bonds, we shall believe.

Beneath the weight of all we've known,
A garden blooms where hope has grown.
For in each heart, the light awaits,
As faded souls renew their fates.

The Liturgy of Grief and Memory

In silent prayer, we gather here,
To honor those we hold so dear.
Each whispered name, a sacred song,
Within our hearts, they still belong.

Through tears we trace the paths once shared,
The laughter breathed, the love declared.
In memories, their spirits glide,
A liturgy where souls abide.

The candles flicker, softly glow,
Illuminating what we know.
In every shadow, light prevails,
A testament that love never fails.

Though sorrow paints the skies with grey,
Their legacy will guide our way.
In every tear, a promise stands,
That time will heal with gentle hands.

With gratitude, we raise our plea,
For all they've given, eternally.
In every breath, we find their grace,
In grief, their love we still embrace.

Ascendancy of Healing Hearts

From broken shards, we rise anew,
In trials faced, a strength we grew.
With every wound, a lesson learned,
In healing light, the hearts return.

The storm may rage, the night may fall,
Yet still we heed the sacred call.
For through the tears, our souls ignite,
Transforming pain to purest light.

Together bound, we journey on,
In unity, the past is gone.
In sacred trust, we venture forth,
To find our worth, to know our worth.

The blossoms bloom where hope is sown,
In every heart, a seed is grown.
With open arms, we share the love,
Embracing peace that comes from above.

So let the healing tide arise,
A chorus sung beneath the skies.
In every heart, a flame will start,
To guide us on, our healing hearts.

Vestiges of Saintly Remembrance

In sacred halls, where echoes dwell,
The whispers weave a timeless spell.
With memories held, we honor grace,
In every heart, their light we trace.

Through trials faced, their courage shines,
In every act, their love aligns.
The vestiges of paths they paved,
In lives renewed, their spirits saved.

The candles burn, a vigil kept,
In silent awe, our sorrows wept.
Yet in the stillness, hope prevails,
For love transcends the fleeting trails.

In every prayer, their names reside,
With gratitude, we feel their guide.
Their teachings linger, softly speak,
In every heart, the strong and meek.

So let us walk in paths of light,
With steadfast hearts, they shine so bright.
In vestiges of love, we find,
A legacy of the divine.

Miracles Among the Fragments

In the broken glass we see,
Reflections of the divine,
Each shard a story whispered,
Of love that's intertwined.

Through the cracks light filters in,
A tapestry of grace,
Though fractured, we find beauty,
In our sacred space.

Hands once trembled with despair,
Now held in prayer's embrace,
In the midst of chaos,
We find a holy place.

Every tear, a precious drop,
Each trial, a step we take,
In the fragments lies a truth,
A path we will awake.

With faith as our foundation,
In unity we stand,
Miracles unfold before,
A guiding, gentle hand.

The Hymn of What Remains

In the silence, echoes hum,
The whispers of the lost,
A hymn that fills the morning,
In the shadows, we are tossed.

Beneath the weight of sorrow,
Hope rises from the ground,
Each note a gentle promise,
In the heart, we are found.

What remains in afterglow,
Is love that can't decay,
Even in our darkest hours,
It guides us on our way.

With every breath, a testament,
To faith that will not break,
In the tapestry of life,
We find the vows we make.

Join the chorus, lift your voice,
In gratitude for grace,
For what remains is sacred,
A timeless, warm embrace.

Reverence in the Wake of Silence

In the quiet, spirits stir,
Whispers float upon the air,
Reverence fills the hollow space,
Every heartbeat a prayer.

When words slip through weary lips,
And shadows start to creep,
Stillness speaks in volumes wide,
Awakens dreams from sleep.

Light breaks softly on the dawn,
Softening the night's despair,
In the hush, divinity,
Awaits in gentle care.

Let each moment breathe in peace,
Wrapped in love's embrace,
In the wake of silence found,
We find our rightful place.

Together bound, we stand as one,
In the reverence we crave,
In the stillness, hearts unite,
And souls the silence save.

The Psalm of Shattered Trust

In the garden, trust was lost,
As petals fell like tears,
Yet, through the cracks, new blooms emerge,
Hearts brave the weight of fears.

Each promise like a fragile leaf,
Fell gently to the ground,
But in the soil, the roots entwined,
Together they are found.

We gather pieces of the past,
And weave a story bright,
In shattered trust, new bonds are forged,
In darkness, we find light.

Through trials, we will cultivate,
A harvest, rich and true,
In vulnerability, we stand,
With love, we will renew.

So let the psalm be sung anew,
In voices brave and strong,
For even in our brokenness,
Together, we belong.

Echoing the Divine in Our Disarray.

In shadows cast by doubt, we roam,
Seeking whispers of a place called home.
Each prayer, a thread within the night,
Echoing grace, igniting our light.

Through tears, our spirits rise and bend,
In chaos, we find the paths to mend.
Divine hands guide our trembling souls,
Restoring fragments, making us whole.

In disarray, we learn to see,
The sacred dance of divinity.
Each heartbeat not in vain, a song,
In harmony, where we belong.

With faith our compass, we embrace,
The beauty held in every trace.
Though storm clouds gather, hope shall soar,
Echoes remind us — love is more.

Awash in grace, we feel the weave,
Divine fabric, we shall believe.
In every crack, the light spills through,
Echoing the divine, pure and true.

Silent Confessions of the Heart

In stillness found, the heart will speak,
Confessions soft, it longs to seek.
Whispers drift on a gentle breeze,
Solace found in divine decrees.

Between the lines of uncharted dreams,
Silence shatters with sacred beams.
Each thought, a prayer, rich and deep,
Nurtured hopes, in silence, we keep.

In shadows cast, the truth resides,
Hidden wounds where love abides.
Our hearts, a garden, wild and free,
Silent confessions — eternity.

The echoes of grace flow through our veins,
Binding hearts in joyful chains.
As tears become the softest part,
We find the voice within the heart.

In the quiet, a melody sings,
Resounding dreams, the spirit clings.
Each moment a step, a divine start,
Navigating silent confessions of the heart.

Sacred Ashes of Lost Dreams

In the embers of what used to be,
We gather strength, and set it free.
Sacred ashes tell ancient tales,
Of hope ignited, of love that prevails.

In the ashes, a truth we find,
Lessons written for heart and mind.
Lost dreams rise, like phoenix' flight,
From sacred dust, they reunite.

With every tear, a seed will bloom,
Transforming darkness into room.
For beauty lies in ashes cast,
The sacred union, future and past.

We stand on ground where hopes have burned,
In sacred silence, we've discerned.
Lost dreams cherished, now reborn,
From sacred ashes, new visions worn.

With open hearts, we nurture light,
In the tapestry of endless night.
In every moment, grace redeems,
From sacred ashes of lost dreams.

The Altar of Our Emptiness

At the altar where we kneel in prayer,
Empty hands raised unto the air.
In our voids, we seek the whole,
Whispering offerings of the soul.

Through silence deep, we learn to see,
The beauty in our vulnerability.
Each heartache a stepping stone,
In emptiness, we are not alone.

We lay our burdens, heavy and bare,
In surrender, we find sacred care.
The journey fraught with shadows still,
Yet love prevails, and hearts will fill.

In echoes found within our plight,
Illuminate the dark with light.
The altar stands, wide open space,
Inviting grace to find its place.

In our emptiness, a call to rise,
The spirit whispers, never disguise.
For in each hollow, grace's embrace,
Awaits us there, our sacred space.

The Sacred Path of Forgiveness

In shadows deep, where hope stands still,
A heart can mend, with gentle will.
The scars of yesterday, now beam,
In light of grace, we softly dream.

With every prayer, a tear is shed,
The weight of sin, like gold, is thread.
In whispered vows, we find our peace,
In seeking truth, our souls release.

Forgiveness blooms like flowers fair,
In tender moments, free from despair.
Each step we take on sacred ground,
Transforming loss, in love unbound.

We walk together, hand in hand,
Upon this path, divinely planned.
Through trials faced, our spirits rise,
In open hearts, the spirit flies.

So let us weave a tapestry,
Of love and light, eternally.
In every dawn, a chance to start,
The sacred path, it guides the heart.

Beneath the Weeping Willows

Beneath the branches, we softly sway,
In whispered prayers, we find our way.
The willow weeps for souls of yore,
And comforts those who seek for more.

In shadows cast, where echoes sleep,
A promise made, we gently keep.
The earth below, our secrets hold,
In silent nights, our stories told.

Nature sings of love and grace,
In every tear, a soft embrace.
With faith as strong as ancient trees,
We bend, but do not break in pleas.

As stars above reflect the light,
We gather hope in darkest night.
Together we stand, side by side,
In unity, our hearts abide.

So let us dwell where peace is found,
Beneath the willows, sacred ground.
With open arms, we greet the morn,
In gentle hearts, new life is born.

The Last Acolyte of Love

In twilight's glow, the candles burn,
A final call, a heart's return.
With open arms, we gather near,
The echoes of love, sweet and clear.

For every soul that walks this way,
Bears burdens carved from yesterday.
Yet in the gloom, a light emerges,
In silent prayers, the spirit surges.

The last acolyte walks the aisle,
In reverence, reflecting style.
With each soft step, the faithful sigh,
As dreams revive and hope runs high.

In every heart, the quest unfolds,
For love transcends, and truth upholds.
Though shadows linger, spirits rise,
In love's embrace, we touch the skies.

So let us cherish every breath,
In life, in love, we conquer death.
For in this tale, the heart will say,
The last acolyte, love's array.

Covenant of Quiet Mourning

In silence deep, where spirits roam,
A covenant forged, to guide us home.
Through whispered winds and fallen leaves,
The heart remembers, though it grieves.

Beneath the stars, we gather round,
In every tear, a blessing found.
The stories shared, a sacred trust,
In love's embrace, we rise from dust.

With each soft sigh, the memories flow,
In quiet moments, love will grow.
For though we part, our souls entwine,
In shadows cast, the light will shine.

Together, we honor what we've lost,
In gentle prayers, we bear the cost.
Yet in this ache, we find the grace,
Of love remembered, a warm embrace.

So let us mourn, yet also sing,
In sacred bonds, the hope we bring.
A covenant made, forever strong,
In quiet mourning, we belong.

In Search of the Absent Spirit

In shadows deep, I wander through,
The echoes of a voice once near.
A whisper calls, yet fades from view,
The missing light, a soul to cheer.

Beneath the stars, a prayer ascends,
For guidance on this winding way.
Through trials faced, my heart contends,
To find the spirit gone astray.

In sacred woods, I search the ground,
For footprints left in days of yore.
Yet silence reigns, no solace found,
The absent spirit I implore.

As dawn breaks, I lift my eyes,
To seek the truth in morning's glow.
Yet all around, the stillness lies,
A haunting peace, a heavy woe.

In faith I tread, though lost, I yearn,
For moments shared, the love I miss.
In every breath, a hope I burn,
To feel again that hallowed bliss.

The Sacred Pilgrimage of Regret

With every step upon this path,
The weight of choices burdens me.
In stillness deep, I feel the wrath,
Of all I lost, what could not be.

A journey forged in tears and sighs,
In shadows past, where folly dwelled.
The sacred truth of whispered lies,
And dreams that time and fate repelled.

I walk alone, the road is long,
Each memory a thorn in skin.
Yet in the heart, there beats a song,
Of grace that flows where pain has been.

Through valleys low and mountains high,
I seek the light, the guiding hand.
To atone for all that passed me by,
In hope, I rise from shifting sand.

In every stone, a tale I find,
Of love and loss, of faith and fear.
This pilgrimage, a testament, blind,
To sacred ground, my spirit near.

A Threnody of Hallowed Longing

Oh mournful heart, what sorrow's song,
Resounds within this empty space?
In every beat, the world feels wrong,
A sacred loss we dare not face.

With tear-stained cheeks, I lift my plea,
To realms above, where spirits soar.
To speak the words that set me free,
From chains of love now seen no more.

In twilight's hush, the shadows loom,
Reminders of what once was bright.
A stolen joy, a pending doom,
The hallowed longing, day and night.

Yet still I walk this path of pain,
In search of solace, light reclaim.
Through parched terrain and softest rain,
Each tear that falls shall bear your name.

So hear me now, O distant star,
As I release this mournful cry.
A threnody of dreams afar,
To hold your essence, never die.

The Remains of a Holy Promise

In solemn vows, once etched in gold,
The promises that time betrayed.
With whispered prayers, my heart consoled,
In sacred trust, our bond displayed.

Yet as the years began to fade,
The echoes of your love grew dim.
A tapestry of hopes we made,
Now hangs in shadows, torn and slim.

The remnants of what used to be,
Lie scattered like the leaves of fall.
A testament to what's not free,
A longing heart still hears your call.

In quiet moments, I reflect,
On all the dreams we wove as one.
Though time has passed, I still project,
The love that shines like morning sun.

The remains of promises once bright,
Shall guide my soul through endless night.
In every tear, a spark of grace,
In memory's arms, I find my place.

Resurrection of the Heart's Echo

In shadows deep where silence dwells,
A whisper stirs, the spirit swells.
From graves of grief, the heart takes flight,
To dance again in morning's light.

With faith as wings, we rise anew,
As dawn unveils the vibrant hue.
Each tear that fell, a sacred seed,
In love's embrace, our souls are freed.

Beneath the weight of darkest night,
Hope flickers soft, a guiding light.
In every sorrow, every pain,
A symphony of joy will reign.

Through trials fierce and tempests strong,
We find the place where we belong.
The echo of our dreams resound,
In every heartbeat, love is found.

And so we walk, our heads held high,
Embracing life, as time goes by.
The resurrection of our core,
A testament to love's great lore.

Seraphim Among the Ashen Remains

In the ruins where shadows creep,
Seraphim awake from their sleep.
With fiery wings and radiant grace,
They guide the lost to a sacred space.

Among the ashes, hope will bloom,
A fragrant whisper dispels the gloom.
In twilight's hush, they sing of peace,
Inviting hearts to find release.

With voices pure, they call us near,
To heal the wounds, to calm the fear.
In every ember, a promise glows,
Of love that mends and gently grows.

In despair's grip, their light breaks through,
With every tear, a prayer rings true.
Among the ashen, they take their stand,
Crafting beauty with loving hand.

So let us rise from sorrow's chain,
Embrace the seraphs, shed the pain.
In unity, we find our song,
Seraphim among us, where we belong.

The Crossroads of What Could Have Been

At twilight's gate, the paths unfold,
Each choice a tale yet to be told.
In quiet whispers, echoes play,
What could have been, in shades of gray.

With every step, the heart may wane,
Yet still we seek to break the chain.
Between the dreams that live and die,
We stand as seekers, asking why.

Regrets like shadows softly blend,
In every turn, we seek a friend.
The crossroads call with gentle plea,
Embrace the now, let worries flee.

Though futures wait, both bright and dim,
Each moment sings the heart's sweet hymn.
In every sigh, a lesson learned,
From choices made, our spirits turned.

So onward still with courage strong,
In faith we trust, we will belong.
To crossroads danced and paths we tread,
To find the light where hope is fed.

Pilgrim's Lament for Grace Lost

A pilgrim walks with weary feet,
Upon the path where sorrow meets.
In search of grace that slipped away,
Through barren lands and skies of gray.

With heavy heart and burdened soul,
Each step a quest to find the whole.
The echoes of a time once bright,
Now linger faint, like fading light.

Through trials faced and shadows cast,
The memories of joy come fast.
For every joy that seemed to gleam,
A tear will fall, a broken dream.

Yet in the stillness of the night,
A whisper forms, a flickering light.
Reminding us, in loss, we find,
A deeper love, a heart aligned.

So pilgrim, weep, but know this grace,
Though moments fade, love leaves its trace.
With every step, let hope be sought,
For every loss shall be for naught.

When the Angels Wept Among Us

When the angels wept among us,
Their tears fell soft like rain.
With gentle whispers they spoke,
Bringing comfort through our pain.

In the stillness of the night,
Their presence filled the air.
We felt the warmth of their light,
Guiding us with tender care.

In shadows cast by doubt,
They danced in silver grace.
Reminding hearts to shout,
In faith, we find our place.

Their songs of hope resound,
Echoing in our dreams.
They lift us from the ground,
And mend our broken seams.

So when despair draws near,
Look closely, you may see.
The angels ever near,
In love, we still believe.

The Chasm Between Existence and Memory

In the chasm vast and deep,
Where echoes softly fade,
We wander through our dreams,
In moments, unafraid.

Memories like ancient trees,
Rooted in sacred ground,
In every whisper, seize,
The love that we have found.

Time weaves a fragile thread,
Between the now and then.
What lives within our head,
Holds truth beyond our ken.

In silence, we shall pray,
For those who've slipped away.
In hearts they ever stay,
Their light will guide our way.

So fear not the divide,
For love shall bridge the gap.
In every tear we've cried,
We find a gentle map.

Traces of You in Every Prayer

In every prayer we raise,
Your name, a sacred sound.
With hopes that dance like rays,
In grace, our hearts are found.

Each whispered thought of you,
A testament of love.
With every breath, it's true,
You linger from above.

The wind carries your voice,
Through valleys, wide and free.
In faith, we make our choice,
To hold your memory.

In trials, we find light,
Your spirit guides our path.
In shadows, you ignite,
A flame that will not quench.

So in this sacred space,
We honor what we've lost.
Your traces, time can't erase,
In love, we bear the cost.

Halo of What Was Once Sacred

Beneath the halo bright,
Of what was once so pure,
We tread with humble hearts,
Seeking solace, we endure.

In every sacred ground,
The whispers of the past.
Echoes of love abound,
And memories that last.

In twilight's tender gaze,
The spirits dance with grace.
Reminding us always,
Of love's eternal place.

Through trials we have faced,
We find our strength in prayer.
In faith, we are embraced,
By light that's always there.

So let the shadows fall,
We walk with heads held high.
In every rise and fall,
Our hearts shall never die.

Seraphs Weeping in Dissonance

In realms above, seraphs sigh,
Their voices break, a mournful cry.
Heaven's tears, like silver rain,
Echoing hearts that feel the pain.

Wings wrapped in shadows, torn apart,
Love and sorrow pierce each heart.
In their lament, a tempest swells,
A hymn of loss, where silence dwells.

What once was bright, now veiled in night,
The glow of faith fades from the light.
In chaos born from yearning's plea,
They search for grace, yet fail to see.

In every note, a ghostly trace,
Of joy transformed in sacred space.
They weave their tales through time's gray mist,
Of hopes once held, now lost, dismissed.

Yet deep within, a flame endures,
Through dissonance, the soul matures.
For in this sorrow, truth takes flight,
Guiding the weary toward the light.

Celestial Fragments of What Once Was

Within the stars, remnants glow,
Echoes of what we used to know.
Whispers dance on cosmic winds,
Where time unravels, and silence begins.

Each fragment glimmers, pale and faint,
Painted dreams of what we can't taint.
Each tale a sigh, a fleeting spark,
In the vastness, where shadows mark.

Faith, a tether to worlds unseen,
In every tear, the spaces in between.
Celestial bodies bleed in grace,
Healing the wounds with a gentle embrace.

From dust we rose, to dust we call,
In transient beauty, we rise and fall.
The heavens weep for moments lost,
In the chase of love, we count the cost.

Yet in these pieces, hope remains,
An ember glowing through our pains.
For even in fragments, spirits soar,
Seeking the unity that was before.

The Temptation of Remembrance

A whisper calls from depths unseen,
The weight of memory, heavy and keen.
In shadows, faces drift and glide,
Rekindling flames we try to hide.

Each thought a thread, pulling us near,
To the echoes of laughter and of fear.
Temptations rise like tides of the sea,
As we wrestle with what used to be.

The heart knows not the bounds of time,
In dreams, we wander beyond the climb.
Yet the ghost of joy is bittersweet,
In remembrance, our souls compete.

In every tear, a story unfolds,
Of love once fierce, now silently cold.
The past, a siren's haunting song,
Resonates deep, where we belong.

Yet we strive to break from the chain,
To find the peace that hides in the rain.
Through remembrance, we seek the dawn,
And dance with shadows until they're gone.

Betrayed by the Light

Once bathed in glory, now blindsided,
By truths we sought but never decided.
The sun casts shadows upon the soul,
A betrayal that takes its toll.

In golden rays, whispers of pain,
A haunting echo of love's disdain.
Illumined by faith, yet lost in strife,
We grasp for meaning, the pulse of life.

What brilliance offered is now a test,
In every flicker, we yearn for rest.
For the light that guides ignites the ache,
As we mourn the dreams that we forsake.

Through every dawn, the shadows creep,
In the wake of hope, secrets keep.
A journey blurred by brilliant rays,
Yet still we seek in countless ways.

Still, we rise from the depths of despair,
Searching for solace in the starlit air.
For though the light may seem to betray,
In love's embrace, we find our way.

Ascension from the Abyss of Us

From the depth where shadows dwell,
We seek the light, our whispered spell.
Voices echo, calling forth,
In faith we rise, reborn in worth.

Through trials fierce, our spirits grow,
With every wound, a chance to glow.
In unity, we find our grace,
Together, we ascend, embrace.

The chains that bind, we cast away,
In fervent prayers, we find our way.
Our hearts, like wings, begin to soar,
Towards the heavens, forevermore.

A path of light, where hope ignites,
In sacred trust, our soul ignites.
Through the tempest, we shall rise,
For love, our compass, guides the skies.

Eternal bonds we forge anew,
In love's embrace, we are the true.
From depths profane to realms divine,
Ascend with faith, our hearts align.

The Gospel of Loneliness

In silence deep, the soul can weep,
Where shadows lie and secrets keep.
A whisper soft, a vacant gaze,
Lost in the heart, the endless maze.

Yet in the stillness, solace blooms,
A gentle light amidst the glooms.
For in the void, reflection starts,
Connecting soul to seeking hearts.

The echoes of a distant prayer,
Remind us we are never bare.
In lonely nights, a spark does gleam,
Hope weaves its fabric into dream.

Embrace the solitude we feel,
For in the pain, our wounds can heal.
The gospel shared in silent cries,
Unites us all beneath the skies.

So walk the path of quiet grace,
In every lonely, sacred place.
The heart will thrum, the spirit yearns,
For every flame, a spirit burns.

Revelations of a Distant Love

Across the miles, your spirit calls,
In twilight realms where silence falls.
A love that spans both time and space,
In dreams we meet, we share our grace.

Your laughter dances on the breeze,
In whispered winds, my soul finds ease.
Each moment shared, though worlds apart,
Ignites the fire within my heart.

Through moonlit nights and sunlit days,
In every thought, your essence stays.
A tapestry of love unfurls,
In every thread, the universe twirls.

Yet distance holds its bitter sting,
In longing's ache, our spirits cling.
But with each dawn, our hope will rise,
For love transcends the earthly ties.

In every star, I see your face,
In each embrace, your sweet grace.
Revelations bloom in sacred light,
A distant love, forever bright.

Epistles to a Lost Beloved

In letters penned with ink of tears,
I send my thoughts throughout the years.
Each word a prayer, each line a plea,
For in this heart, you dwell with me.

The pages whisper tales of old,
Of love once warm, now left untold.
In memories etched, your laughter rings,
A symphony that sorrow brings.

With every sunset, shadows play,
Reminding me of love's bright day.
I write to you through night's embrace,
To feel again your tender grace.

Yet, distance looms, and time must part,
Our souls united, still, apart.
In every stroke, my heart lays bare,
An epistle forged in love and care.

So take these words, let them be known,
A testament to love's true throne.
With hope as ink, and faith as light,
In every letter, you take flight.

Communion with Ghosts of Affection

In whispers soft, they call my name,
Echoes of love, lingering flame.
In shadows cast by a fading light,
Hearts entwined in the still of night.

Their laughter dances in the breeze,
Memories wrapped in sacred ease.
Together we share this holy space,
With tender thoughts, we find our grace.

Each sigh a prayer, each tear a plea,
In the quiet fold of eternity.
Bound by the threads of what has been,
United forever, souls intertwined.

In this communion, love remains,
Beyond the veil, where hope sustains.
With gentle hands, we craft our way,
Through realms of light where spirits play.

Thus, in each heart, a ghost shall dwell,
A story of affection, we weave so well.
For in remembrance, our spirits soar,
In timeless dance, forevermore.

The Sacred Space of Reminiscence

Beneath the arch of sacred skies,
We gather here, where memory lies.
A tapestry woven with threads of old,
In whispers and sighs, our tales unfold.

Candles flicker, illuminating the past,
In every shadow, love's shadows cast.
A sanctuary of silent grace,
Where every moment finds its place.

With hands uplifted, we seek the light,
In the sacred space of day and night.
Reflections shimmer, emotions swell,
In the harmony that words can't tell.

Songs of the heart, they rise anew,
In solemn vows, our spirits grew.
Each fragment of joy and pain we hold,
In the sacred space, our truth unfolds.

In this hallowed ground, we meet again,
In every heartbeat, amidst the pain.
Together we stand, bonded and free,
In loving memory, eternally.

Stained Glass Memories

Fragments of life in colors bold,
Windows to stories that softly unfold.
Each hue a heartbeat, each shade a prayer,
In the stained glass light, hope lingers there.

Fleeting moments caught in time,
Captured beauty, both pure and sublime.
Through prisms of sorrow, joy can gleam,
In every shadow, there's a dream.

Broken pieces, yet art they make,
In every fracture, new paths awake.
A mosaic of love, light, and despair,
In these memories, we find our share.

They guide our hearts, these colorful frames,
Forging our spirits, igniting our flames.
In the tapestry of life that we weave,
Stained glass memories, we believe.

And thus we cherish the light we gain,
From shards of life, both joy and pain.
Together they shimmer and brightly shine,
In stained glass wisdom, our souls align.

The Beatitudes of Brokenness

Blessed are those who mourn the lost,
For in their tears, true love embossed.
Through shadows deep, they find their way,
To healing whispers at break of day.

Blessed are hearts that bear the scars,
For in their struggles, shine like stars.
In brokenness, the spirit grows,
From ashes rise a flower that knows.

Blessed are the humble, those who bend,
For in their grace, they find the end.
In letting go, they learn to soar,
With wings of faith, they seek for more.

Blessed are the seekers, lost in pain,
In their searching hearts, wisdom reigns.
For every fracture holds a key,
To deeper truths that set them free.

And in their journey through the night,
They find the dawn, a softest light.
With every step, a promise made,
In the beatitudes, hope won't fade.

Sacramental Tears and Broken Vows

In whispered prayers, our sorrows flow,
Each tear a sign of love and woe.
Promises made, now slip like sand,
Yet still we seek Your guiding hand.

Hearts once joined, now torn apart,
In sacred moments, we restart.
With every mournful, trembling cry,
We find the strength to rise and fly.

Broken vows, yet grace remains,
In every loss, Your love sustains.
Through veils of pain, Your light will shine,
In every heart, Your peace divine.

Rebuild the bridges washed away,
We seek the dawn of a new day.
In sorrow's depth, we find a way,
To honor love, though it may sway.

So let our tears, like rivers, run,
To cleanse the wounds, make us as one.
For in our hearts, You dwell so near,
Transforming pain to promises dear.

The Light that Fades into Shadow

In twilight's hush, the shadows creep,
Soft whispers of the dreams we keep.
As daylight wanes, our hope takes flight,
Seeking solace in the night.

With every breath, the echoes fade,
Yet faith remains, a serenade.
For in the depths of darkest sorrow,
We find the strength to greet tomorrow.

The light that flickers, dim yet strong,
Guides hearts that feel they don't belong.
In every crack, a chance to grow,
In silent prayers, Your love will show.

Though shadows loom, we seek Your face,
In quiet trust, we find our grace.
For even when the night is long,
We'll sing the everlasting song.

O Silent One, in dusk's embrace,
Illuminate the hidden space.
With every step, let burdens lift,
In darkness, Lord, Your love's the gift.

Portraits of Grace Amidst Sorrow

In frames of grief, we find the light,
Each moment captured, shining bright.
Through tears we paint our stories true,
With every brushstroke, we come anew.

Though sadness drapes like velvet night,
Your love ignites our inner sight.
In portraits raw, we lay bare our souls,
Trusting in You to make us whole.

The beauty blooms from brokenness,
In every ache, we find Your rest.
Through fragile hearts, Your strength will flow,
In quiet whispers, peace will grow.

As seasons change, our lives unfold,
With every story, we are bold.
In grace, we learn the art of loss,
To honor love, no matter the cost.

So paint our tears with colors bright,
Transform our shadows into light.
For in these frames, we see Your plan,
In every moment, Your love will stand.

Sanctity in the Midst of Grief

In moments dark, where sorrow hides,
Your presence dwells, our pain confides.
With every heartbeat, whispers bloom,
Sanctity found amidst the gloom.

Through shattered dreams and crumbled hopes,
In grieving hearts, Your mercy copes.
You cradle us in gentle arms,
Transforming pain to sacred charms.

For grief, a path to deeper grace,
We seek Your love in every space.
In echoes soft, our spirits soar,
With every loss, we trust You more.

The sacred dance of joy and tears,
We trace the steps through all our fears.
In every struggle, we discern,
The lessons taught, the paths we yearn.

So teach us, Lord, to cherish pain,
In every loss, Your love remains.
For in our grief, we find the light,
A testament to love's great fight.

A Rosary of Stolen Moments

In whispers shared beneath the stars,
Days slip by like fleeting hours.
We count our dreams like beads of light,
Grace in the silence, hope takes flight.

Each moment treasured, a sacred prayer,
Fingers clasped in the soft night air.
Stolen time, a divine embrace,
Heaven's laughter fills this space.

The sun dips low, a promise made,
Joy in shadows, love won't fade.
With every breath, we hold the truth,
In the journey we reclaim our youth.

Here within this sacred trust,
Hearts entwined, it's love we must.
Soft echoes in the velvet night,
In every heartbeat, pure delight.

Each stolen moment, a tender kiss,
In the silence, we find our bliss.
Together we write this holy song,
In the tapestry of love, we belong.

Chronicles of Grace and Grief

In shadows linger tales unsaid,
Where grace and grief in silence tread.
Hearts bend low, yet rise again,
In the sorrow, we shall wane.

Through every tear, a blessing blooms,
In every trial, the spirit grooms.
On the altar of loss, we find release,
In memories sweet, our souls find peace.

A hymn of healing, soft and clear,
In the echoes of pain, love is near.
With every chapter, scars become stars,
A testament written in healing bars.

Together we walk through valleys deep,
In faith we gather, in trust we keep.
The sun will rise, bringing light anew,
In every heart, a story true.

Between joy and sorrow, life's thin line,
In sacred spaces, we intertwine.
As chronicles weave, we embrace the whole,
In grace and grief, we find our soul.

The Penance of Heartstrings Frayed

In tapestry woven with threads of pain,
Each heartstring frayed bears love's refrain.
Through trials faced, we seek atonement,
In the wreckage, find our own empowerment.

The weight of sorrow, a heavy shroud,
Yet in every struggle, we are proud.
For every wound, a story spun,
Bringing light where darkness shunned.

In quietude, the spirit prays,
Transforming anguish into praise.
With each confession, our burdens lift,
In penance, we discover the gift.

Through broken chords, we learn to sing,
In the wreckage, grace takes wing.
Love transcends, and hope remains,
In the process, freedom gains.

So let us gather, hearts laid bare,
In the penance, our spirits share.
For in this journey, frayed yet true,
We find redemption in love anew.

Ashes to Ascension

From ashes cold, we rise once more,
In the depths, we unlock the door.
Embers whisper of times gone by,
In the fire, our spirits fly.

Through loss we learn, through pain we grow,
In twilight's grasp, the truth we know.
Each trial faced, a lesson learned,
In every lit path, the heart discerned.

In moments dark, a guiding flame,
In struggle's grip, we call his name.
From rubble's grasp, our voices swell,
In faith reborn, we rise, we dwell.

Lifted high in ascension's grace,
We find our strength in every place.
Through skies of blue where angels fly,
From ashes formed, our spirits sigh.

Together we soar on wings of time,
In the journey grand, our spirits climb.
To heights unknown, we trust the way,
In the beauty of dawn, we greet the day.

The Last Supper of Our Affection

In the quiet glow of twilight's grace,
We gather close, a sacred space.
Bread of unity upon our tears,
Wine of memories, shared through years.

Hands clasped in prayer, we seek the light,
Echoes of love that banish the night.
Each morsel carries a whispered prayer,
Binding our spirits, a bond so rare.

The table set with humility's peace,
In every bite, our burdens cease.
Voices rise in a soft refrain,
Together we heal the heart's deep pain.

As shadows dance and time does fade,
We honor the ties that fate has made.
In this last supper, our hearts extend,
For love is the feast that has no end.

May this moment linger in sacred trust,
An echo of faith, profound and just.
With every sip, our spirits soar,
At the last supper, forevermore.

Reflections in the Waters of Remorse

Still waters whisper secrets untold,
Mirroring the past as it unfolds.
With trembling hands, I dip my soul,
In currents dark, where shadows console.

Each ripple carries a sigh of pain,
Regrets take flight, like whispers of rain.
Drowned in silence, I seek the shore,
Yearning to cleanse what I can't restore.

Among the reeds, lost thoughts entwine,
A broken heart waits for a sign.
In the echoes, I find clarity,
Reflections of faith guiding me free.

The waters speak of mercy and grace,
In their depths, I long to embrace.
With every wave, I feel reborn,
From guilt's tight grip, my spirit is torn.

Beneath the surface, new hopes arise,
Fleeting shadows replaced by the wise.
In the stillness, I learn to forgive,
For in remorse, the soul must live.

Covenant of the Diaspora Heart

In far-off lands where ancestors wandered,
A promise forged, where love has pondered.
With every step on foreign ground,
Echoes of home in the lost are found.

Threads of connection weave through the years,
In struggles faced, we shed our fears.
Hearts adrift, yet bound in faith,
In every sorrow, a joy we wraith.

Through trials faced, a tapestry spun,
In unity's light, we nurture the one.
With ink of resilience, we write our tale,
In distant shores, our voices prevail.

The songs of our fathers guide our way,
In every night, there's a breaking day.
The diaspora heart beats strong and free,
In every beat, a sweet unity.

So let us gather, both near and far,
Our souls entwined, like the evening star.
In this covenant, our spirits unite,
Through love's embrace, we find our light.

The Last Testament of Departed Dreams

In the quiet dawn where shadows lay,
Whispers of dreams begin to sway.
A testament borne from heart's own quest,
In the silence, our hopes find rest.

With every heartbeat, memories bloom,
Filling the air with absent perfume.
Voices of lost ones echo in time,
Guiding the weary with love's sweet rhyme.

Each dream departed, a lesson learned,
In the ashes of longing, passion burned.
Yet from the void, new visions rise,
A testament sung in the skies.

Let not the sorrow define the soul,
For in the darkness, we seek the whole.
In every farewell, a promise stays,
In dreams that linger, love never strays.

So let us cherish the moments we've known,
In the garden of hope, seeds have been sown.
The last testament, love always redeems,
In the hearts of the brave, live the dreams.

Beneath the Stars of Our Farewell

Beneath the stars, we stand in grace,
The night whispers soft in our embrace.
Each twinkling light, a tear of gold,
A tale of love that shall be told.

With every breath, the heavens sigh,
As shadows dance, and moments fly.
In sacred silence, hearts entwined,
A bond unbroken, truly divine.

As dawn shall break with tender light,
We promise skies, though far from sight.
Love's echoes linger in the air,
Forever felt, beyond compare.

In parting's kiss, the stars hold tight,
A guiding force through darkest night.
With faith as our lantern, we shall find,
The path of love, though far combined.

Beneath the veil of cosmic dreams,
United still, despite the seams.
In every heart, a piece we keep,
Awake in spirit, never sleep.

Reverent Silence of Parting

In reverent silence, we draw near,
Embracing whispers, soft and clear.
The sacred bond does not unwind,
In parting's grace, love is enshrined.

With gentle hands, we hold the night,
Each moment brief, yet shining bright.
The echoes of your voice remain,
In every prayer, a sweet refrain.

While paths may part, our souls persist,
With faith, a map that can't be missed.
In sacred spaces, we reside,
In every heartbeat, love abides.

The weight of sorrow, light we bear,
With whispered hopes, we weave a prayer.
And as we stand in twilight's glow,
The grace of love begins to show.

In stillness now, we raise the call,
In every tear, we rise, we fall.
As stars align in mournful sky,
In reverent silence, we won't die.

Celestial Remnants of Love's Fire

In celestial realms, our love burns bright,
Remnants glowing, piercing the night.
With every spark, a memory glows,
In sacred warmth, the spirit knows.

Through trials faced, we stand as one,
The fire ignites, though time has spun.
With ashes soft, our journey's told,
In every ember, a heart of gold.

As constellations trace the skies,
Our love, a beacon that never dies.
With passion's flame, we won't relent,
In every silence, love's scent is lent.

In twilight's hush, we hear the song,
A melody where we belong.
In celestial dance, our spirits soar,
With remnants bright, we seek for more.

As night unveils its tapestry,
We write our tale in harmony.
With open hearts, we burn anew,
In love's embrace, forever true.

The Mirror of Distant Souls

In the mirror of distant souls we gaze,
Reflecting light in myriad ways.
With every glance, the truth unfurls,
A sacred dance through timeless swirls.

The stars align in paths unknown,
Two hearts entwined, yet never alone.
Each whispered prayer, a bridge to span,
In love's embrace, we truly can.

With every breath, a silent vow,
To cherish the present, here and now.
In solemn stillness, wisdom flows,
As distant souls, our love still grows.

With threads of fate, we weave our tale,
A tapestry rich, where none will fail.
In every heartbeat, echoes blend,
In love's great journey, there is no end.

Through the mirror's gaze, we find our peace,
In every challenge, our hearts increase.
For in this bond, we shall remain,
In the mirror of souls, forever claimed.

Shadows Beneath the Celestial Veil

Under the heavens, whispers rise,
In shadows deep, where faith complies.
Stars tremble in the silent night,
Guiding souls toward the light.

A path unseen, with hope we tread,
In every prayer, where spirits wed.
Veils of grace, a touch divine,
In sacred trust, our hearts entwine.

Clouds gather, holding dreams anew,
In sacred silence, a promise true.
Shadows dance, yet we hold fast,
For every trial, we will outlast.

Beneath the moon's soft, watchful gaze,
We find our strength in heartfelt praise.
With every breath, a hymn we sing,
To the joy and solace love can bring.

Eternal skies, our witness fair,
In every heart, a silent prayer.
Together bound, through joys and strife,
We walk in faith, embracing life.

Prayers in the Ruins of Us

In crumbling walls where echoes dwell,
We find the truth in a broken spell.
Amid the dust, our spirits rise,
With whispered hopes, we touch the skies.

Each stone recalls the love we knew,
In shadows cast by hearts so true.
Through trials faced, our vision clears,
In silent prayers, we shed our fears.

The remnants speak of joy and pain,
In every tear, a golden chain.
Together lost, yet still we seek,
In gentleness, our hearts still speak.

From ashes born, a flame ignites,
Through bitter nights, we find our rights.
In ruins deep, we build anew,
With faith the bond that sees us through.

In every prayer, a chance to mend,
From loss we rise, on love we depend.
In the ruins left, we sow our seeds,
For in our hearts, the spirit feeds.

Hymns for the Departed Heart

In twilight's glow, the silence weeps,
For every soul that gently sleeps.
A hymn ascends on every sigh,
For those we hold, who now must fly.

In every note, a memory calls,
In echoes soft, the spirit falls.
With wings of light, they soar above,
Wrapping us still in endless love.

Through tender verses, we remember,
In faded warmth of a waning ember.
Each heartbeat sings a sacred tune,
Beneath the watchful, silver moon.

Though parted now, they're never far,
In whispered dreams, they guide the star.
In love's embrace, the bond remains,
Through every joy, through every pain.

So let us chant these hymns alive,
In every heart, the love will thrive.
For though they've gone from sight today,
In spirit's realm, they always stay.

The Lament of Our Broken Covenant

In shadows cast, our vow lays bare,
The echoes linger in whispered prayer.
We stand alone, with hearts contrite,
In search of peace, forsaking fight.

With every breath, a heart's demise,
In promises lost, where silence cries.
Reaching out, we seek to mend,
In faith, together once again.

Yet storms have raged, and tempests tore,
The fabric fine of love's sweet lore.
In fractured nights, we weep as one,
For the bond that left us all undone.

Beneath the stars, we vow to strive,
To heal the wounds and bring alive.
With every tear, a chance to grow,
In planted seeds, our hearts will sow.

So listen, love, as we retract,
In this lament, we will not lack.
For every scar, a story told,
In broken light, our truth unfolds.

Prayer Beads of Memories Past

In the quiet of dawn, I count each bead,
Whispers of grace, in silence they plead.
Threads of the past, interwoven and tight,
Each moment a prayer, from darkness to light.

Traces of laughter, in echoes they stay,
A tapestry woven of hope and dismay.
With every soft touch, the memories bloom,
A fragrant reminder that banishes gloom.

In shadows of sorrow, the blessings unfold,
Lessons of love, in the stories retold.
As twilight descends, I kneel in my grace,
Finding the solace in every embrace.

The beads roll like time, each moment a pearl,
Drifting through life in a divine swirl.
With faith as my guide, I offer my plea,
For peace in the storm, for strength to be free.

As night wraps its arms, I whisper my dreams,
To the stars above, where eternity gleams.
With prayer beads of memories, I find my way,
To the heart of existence, where love holds sway.

Cursed by the Echo of Foregone Joys

In the silence of night, the shadows call me,
Whispers of laughter, that used to be free.
Cursed by the echoes, they haunt like a ghost,
A bittersweet memory, I cherish the most.

Faded images dance on an old, dusty wall,
Moments of glory now tethered in thrall.
With every heartbeat, the past aches with sting,
As joy that once flourished is now but a wing.

Beneath the moonlight, the dreams softly fade,
Promises broken, in the darkness, they wade.
Yet in the deep sorrow, a flicker of grace,
Reminds me of love, in the lostness, I trace.

Paths lined with laughter, now overgrown weeds,
Faint whispers of hope, like delicate seeds.
Yet still I wander, through memories of old,
Searching for warmth in the echoes untold.

Each night I return to the echoes that bind,
To find a new dawn in the darkness confined.
Though cursed by the past, I seek to rejoice,
In the promise of healing, I find my own voice.

A Solitary Pilgrim's Revelation

Beneath the vast sky, I walk my own road,
A pilgrim of faith, with a heart like a code.
In the solitude found, revelations ignite,
The whispers of shadows, awaken my sight.

With each step I take, the burdens release,
In the stillness of spirit, I find my own peace.
Mountains stand tall, yet my soul feels the lift,
Nature's embrace is a sacred, sweet gift.

I speak to the stars, my prayers on the breeze,
In the rustle of leaves, I find answers with ease.
The path may be lonely, but light guides my way,
In the heart of the journey, I learn how to stay.

Through valleys of doubt, in shadows I tread,
Yet each footfall whispers the paths I have led.
With wisdom unfolding, like pages I turn,
A solitary pilgrim, with passion I yearn.

The journey is sacred, the struggle my grace,
In the tapestry woven, I find my true place.
With open heart, I seek the divine,
In the depths of my spirit, soul's juncture align.

The Garden Where Shadows Linger

In the garden's green heart, where shadows entwine,
Whispers of secrets dwell soft like fine wine.
Petals of wisdom fall, gentle as night,
Crafting a canvas where darkness finds light.

Stillness surrounds me, a hymn on the breeze,
Nature's embrace, an ancient reprise.
With every soft rustle, the past brushes near,
In the silence I find, a deep-rooted fear.

Echoes of sunlight dance on the ground,
In the garden of longing, such beauty is found.
Though shadows may linger, they teach and they mold,
Carving the stories that silently unfold.

With every bloom fragile, a memory thrives,
The garden recalls all the lost, yet survives.
In soft, secret corners, the heart learns to trust,
In the shadows of sorrow, there's beauty in dust.

As dusk turns to night, I wander and wait,
For the whispers of dreams that shall open the gate.
In the garden where shadows gather and sway,
I find a reminder that night turns to day.

The Hopeful Penitence of Time

In the stillness of night, we seek your grace,
Bending hearts and knees in humble embrace.
Wounds of the past, they whisper and call,
Yet, in your mercy, we dare not to fall.

With each tick of the clock, hope springs anew,
Forgiveness like morning, bright and true.
A journey of souls, through shadows and light,
We rise from the ashes, prepared for the fight.

The tears that have fallen, they cleanse and renew,
In the garden of faith, your love breaks through.
Time holds the key, our penance refined,
With each step we take, your presence reminds.

From rivers of sorrow, we draw strength to sing,
Each heartbeat a prayer, to you, we cling.
For in the embrace of your endless embrace,
The hopeful are gathered, redeemed by your grace.

So let us rejoice in this moment divine,
For hope is the gift, and through you, it shines.
With thankful hearts, we gather and pray,
In the hopeful penitence of today.

Broken Hallelujahs

In the chasms of silence, we raise our song,
With voices like whispers, that carry along.
For life's bitter trials have battered our chords,
Yet still in our hearts, we sing of the Lord.

Through valleys of shadows, we wander far,
With broken hallelujahs, like a distant star.
Each note tells a story of loss and of grace,
Reminding us gently of love's warm embrace.

We gather the fragments, with faith as our glue,
Transforming our sorrows to something anew.
In the ashes of pain, the fire still burns,
As each broken shout, in our souls, returns.

Let the echoes of struggle bring forth blissful praise,
In moments of darkness, his light still stays.
Each tear that we shed is a seed in the ground,
With faith in the future, hope will surround.

So here we stand, flawed yet refined,
With hearts full of music, in unison aligned.
With broken hallelujahs, the heavens will see,
That even in trials, we are truly free.

Sacred Echoes of Yesterday

In the tapestry woven, our stories reside,
Threads of devotion, where faith will abide.
With sacred echoes of yesterday's light,
We gather in prayer, united and bright.

The whispers of wisdom, like breezes that pass,
Guide our weary hearts through the shadowy grass.
Each lesson a beacon, each moment a thread,
In the fabric of grace, our spirits are led.

Remember the journeys our elders have faced,
The courage that blossomed in trials embraced.
Each echo a promise, a silent refrain,
Revealing the blessings that arise from pain.

Through valleys of sorrow, through mountains of hope,
We stand on the shoulders of those who have coped.
Their laughter, their tears, their prayers intertwine,
As sacred echoes guide us to the divine.

So let us give thanks for the paths that we tread,
For the love and the wisdom that steady our head.
May we carry their light into days yet to be,
With sacred echoes shaping our destiny.

The Saints of Our Darkened Days

In the shadows we gather, where troubles reside,
The saints of our darkened days walk by our side.
With faith unyielding, they shine through the night,
Their love like a beacon, a guiding light.

For every burden we carry alone,
There's strength in their whispers; we're never on our
own.
In moments of anguish, their courage will stay,
Reminding us gently to seek the right way.

Their stories of struggle, they speak to our souls,
In every heartache, their memory consoles.
With arms open wide, they embrace our despair,
Transforming our darkness to hope, pure and rare.

Let the saints of our past lead us through the storm,
Their wisdom a shelter, their love keeps us warm.
In times of confusion, their voices ring clear,
They lift us from sorrow, and banish our fear.

So here we find strength in the journey we share,
The saints of our darkened days are always there.
Together we'll rise, with courage displayed,
In unity's grace, we will never be frayed.

Light in the Labyrinth of Loss

In shadows deep, the heart does wane,
A flicker shines through grief and pain.
With whispered prayers, our spirits soar,
Seeking solace forevermore.

In the winding paths, the echoes sound,
Memories linger, love unbound.
Each step we take, a sacred trace,
Guided by light, in this dark place.

Through thickets wild, the thorns do cling,
Yet hope emerges, vibrant spring.
A lantern glows, a guiding star,
Illuminating just how far.

In faith we walk, despite the night,
Hand in hand, we seek the light.
The labyrinth fades, the heart renews,
In love's embrace, we will not lose.

Each loss a lesson, each tear a prayer,
In the silence, we find the care.
For in the dark, we shall arise,
Embracing love that never dies.

Faith Lost in the Wilderness

In barren lands, where shadows play,
I wander lost, my faith astray.
The sky above is gray and cold,
A tale of hope that feels untold.

Each whispering breeze recalls a prayer,
Yet silence falls, as I despair.
The path ahead, obscured by doubt,
But deep within, the spark burns out.

In dunes of sorrow, I tread alone,
Each grain a burden, each step a moan.
Yet in this void, a soft voice sighs,
Reminding me of unseen ties.

Through trials faced in endless night,
A flame ignites, rekindled light.
In wilderness wide, my heart still yearns,
For faith renewed, as the spirit learns.

So in this journey, I will roam,
For even lost, I seek my home.
And though the wilderness seems to shun,
Faith's gentle whisper has just begun.

Reflections on a Disrupted Covenant

In shadows cast by broken vows,
I search for truth that love allows.
The sacred bond, now torn apart,
Leaves echoes deep within the heart.

Once woven tight in threads of grace,
Now silent tears, an empty space.
Promises whispered in softer times,
Remain as haunting, unfinished rhymes.

Yet in the stillness, wisdom calls,
Though shattered dreams, the spirit sprawls.
Reflections dance upon the stream,
Revealing paths beyond the dream.

For every fracture holds a light,
A chance to rise, to take the flight.
In brokenness, a chance to mend,
To find the love that will not end.

So let us tread, though frail we be,
Each step a path to destiny.
And in the ruins of hope's lament,
We find new covenants, heaven-sent.

The Graveyard of Old Promises

In twilight's grip, the shadows creep,
Where dreams lie low, in silence deep.
The stones are cold, the names worn thin,
Echoes of hopes where love had been.

Here lies the trust, buried with care,
Among the whispers in the air.
Each sigh a ghost of paths once walked,
In gardens lush, where once we talked.

Yet life persists, though promises fade,
In memories crafted, unafraid.
For in this graveyard, seeds still grow,
From soil enriched by love's own glow.

Though old vows linger in fleeting sighs,
In sacred earth, the spirit flies.
Renewed by time, the heart finds peace,
And from the past, sweet joy's release.

So let us cherish the paths we've trod,
In every loss, we still find God.
For in this graveyard, love transcends,
Old promises morph, but never end.

The Last Psalm of Our Union

In shadows deep, we find our way,
A bond unbroken, come what may.
With whispers soft, the spirits call,
In hallowed halls, we stand, not fall.

Through trials faced, we stand as one,
Beneath the gaze of setting sun.
Each heartbeat echoes, love and grace,
In every tear, a sacred trace.

When darkness looms, our faith will shine,
With every prayer, our hope entwined.
Across the ages, truths we seek,
In sacred verses, hearts will speak.

The heavens weep, yet we rejoice,
In union strong, we claim our voice.
As stars align, our spirits soar,
In the last psalm, we are much more.

So hold me close, in light and dread,
For in our love, the past is wed.
Together onward, ever bold,
In sacred whispers, life unfolds.

Celestial Dust and Soul's Retreat

Among the stars, our dreams take flight,
In cosmic dust, we seek the light.
With every sigh, a prayer ascends,
In quiet realms, where spirit mends.

From earthly binds, we long to part,
In sacred spaces, find our heart.
The universe whispers, soft and wise,
In morning's glow, our souls arise.

Each raindrop falls, a promise made,
In nature's arms, our fears do fade.
Celestial rhythms, pure and true,
In every breath, a world anew.

To walk in faith, through vast expanse,
With every step, the stars will dance.
In gentle breezes, we shall hear,
The call of love, forever near.

So let us wander, hand in hand,
In soul's retreat, we understand.
Through timeless echoes, we shall find,
In cosmic love, our hearts entwined.

Faithful in the Wake of Sorrow

When shadows fall, and hope seems lost,
In faithful hearts, we count the cost.
Each tear that falls, a seed of grace,
In trials faced, we find our place.

With every sunrise, light will break,
In whispered prayers, the earth will shake.
Through storms we tread, hand in hand,
In faith and love, forever stand.

For in the depths, our spirits rise,
In every silence, sacred ties.
With courage strong, we face the night,
In tender glow, we seek the light.

When grief surrounds, we gather near,
In shared embrace, we shed our fear.
To lift each other, bear the load,
In faith's embrace, we find the road.

So let us sing, through darkened days,
In faithful hearts, our love shall blaze.
For through the sorrow, joy will bloom,
In every shadow, light will loom.

Rapture's Fractured Reflection

In mirrors dim, we see the light,
A fractured path, yet hearts take flight.
Through broken dreams, we seek the whole,
In every echo, calls the soul.

With whispered truths, our spirits blend,
In rapture's grip, we find a friend.
Each moment dear, a fleeting glance,
In love's embrace, we find our chance.

When silence reigns, the heart will speak,
Through trials faced, it's strength we seek.
In sacred dances, joy and pain,
In fractured pieces, love remains.

So gather close, in twilight's hue,
In every heartbeat, I find you.
The past may break, yet hope will mend,
In rapture's light, our souls transcend.

Through every tear, our truth will shine,
In shattered dreams, our love divine.
For in the mirror, through the night,
Reflections sing, we are the light.

Elysium Lost Among Heartstrings

In gardens where the spirit roams,
The echoes of sweet hymns arise,
Yet shadows dance where love once bloomed,
A whisper lost beneath the skies.

Beneath the tangled vines of fate,
We search for solace, hope in pain,
Yet every tear, a heavy weight,
Each heartbeat sings a soft refrain.

The stars align in silent grace,
A testament to dreams we chase,
Yet fleeting joy may leave its trace,
In hearts that yearn for love's embrace.

Oh, Elysium, where have you gone?
Among the heartstrings, tied in knots,
We seek the light that lingers on,
But find the darkness fills our thoughts.

With every breath, we hold our fate,
In memory, sweet and bittersweet,
In love's embrace, we light the way,
Yet still, we mourn what's incomplete.

The Final Benediction of Us

In silence deep, where whispers dwell,
Our hearts aligned in sacred trust,
We gather 'neath the love's soft spell,
A tender prayer in ancient dust.

With hands entwined, we face the dawn,
In twilight's glow, we bid farewell,
To dreams once bright, now gently drawn,
A final kiss, our souls compel.

The echoes of our laughter fade,
Yet in the stillness, grace remains,
A benediction softly laid,
In memories, love's endless chains.

As seasons turn and rivers flow,
We live the moments, sweet and pure,
In every tear, new strength will grow,
Enduring love, a blessed cure.

When shadows fall and time stands still,
We hold the faith within our hearts,
In love's embrace, we find our will,
Through every end, a new love starts.

Sacrifice to the Silence

In the quiet hour we bow our heads,
With whispered vows that fade like night,
We offer dreams upon the threads,
Of destiny, our hearts' delight.

Each sacrifice, a gift of grace,
In silence, burdens soft and light,
Our souls entwined, we seek a place,
Where love can bloom, forever bright.

Yet in the stillness, echoes call,
Of hopes we laid upon the stone,
In every tear and shadowed fall,
The light of truth is carved alone.

Through trials deep, we forge our way,
A testament to love's embrace,
In sacrifice, our spirits sway,
As silence holds us, warm and trace.

So let us walk this path of peace,
With hearts ablaze in gentle fire,
In every breath, our love won't cease,
A song of loss, and yet, desire.

Hymn of the Forgotten Sanctuary

In shadows where the memories dwell,
A sanctuary lost from time,
We gather still, our hearts compel,
To sing the hymns of love sublime.

The stones may weep with tales untold,
Yet spirits rise in soaring grace,
Within these walls, the brave and bold,
We find our strength, a warm embrace.

Each sacred breath, a promise made,
In quietude, the echoes ring,
For every heart that once had strayed,
We find our way in love's sweet spring.

As twilight falls on hidden streams,
We tread the path of those before,
In love's embrace, we weave our dreams,
A hymn of hope, forevermore.

Through every trial we shall rise,
In harmony, our voices blend,
With faith renewed, we touch the skies,
In this sanctuary, love won't end.

Resonance of Hope in Despair

In shadows cast by sorrow's reign,
A flicker glows that breaks the chain.
The whispers call through darkest nights,
With faith as wings that reach new heights.

Upon the path of weary tread,
A sacred drum beats hope instead.
Each teardrop quenches parched ground's plea,
For dawn will rise, and hearts will see.

When doubts may cling like winter's frost,
The loving hand knows not of loss.
With every breath, His grace we find,
A lightened load, a steadfast mind.

In prayer, our spirits intermingle,
Through trials faced, our souls are single.
Resonance sings in hearts' despair,
For love endures, a timeless prayer.

So, let us stand where shadows fall,
With voices raised, we heed the call.
In every heart, a sacred spark,
Resonance shines within the dark.

Benevolent Ruins of Our Sacred Bond

In crumbled stone, a tale resides,
Of love that built where faith abides.
Though walls may shake and silence reign,
Our spirits rise, with hope's refrain.

Beneath the weight of shattered dreams,
The river flows with healing streams.
In brokenness, a beauty's found,
The whispers of the lost resound.

Among the ruins, prayers ascend,
Each craggy path, a faithful friend.
Together we mend with gentle hands,
Constructing dreams on shifting sands.

The heart recalls what eyes can't see,
Our sacred bond shall ever be.
In every scar, a story told,
Of love's resilience, brave and bold.

So let us walk in twilight's glow,
With faith anew, our spirits flow.
In benevolent ruins, we discover,
The strength that lives in one another.

Celestial Dawns from Twilight's End

As dusk embraces night's soft fold,
The universe in silence holds.
In stillness deep, the stars align,
A whisper speaks beyond the pine.

From twilight's end, new visions rise,
In luminous hues that fill the skies.
The dawn reflects on eyes anew,
A promise made, forever true.

With hearts alight in morning's grace,
We touch the heavens face to face.
Each breath a hymn, each step a prayer,
In unity, our souls lay bare.

Celestial calls in softest tones,
Guide weary hearts to faith's deep homes.
In every heartbeat, a world reborn,
From twilight's end, new hope is sworn.

So as the sun brings warmth again,
We'll walk in light, dispelling pain.
Celestial dawns, a sacred start,
Illuminating every heart.

Harvesting the Fractured Heart

In fields of sorrow, seeds we sow,
From fractured soil, new blossoms grow.
Each wound a chance for grace to mend,
In brokenness, we find our blend.

Through aching roots, the spirit weaves,
In love's embrace, we learn and leave.
The harvest time calls forth our fight,
Transforming pain to purest light.

With tender hands, we gather round,
Each cherished soul, a sacred sound.
In unity, our strength's displayed,
For every heart that's gently swayed.

The fractured pieces create a song,
In harmony where we belong.
Together we rise, fierce and whole,
Harvesting gifts within each soul.

So let us toil in hope's bright field,
With every trial, our fate is sealed.
For in the act of love's great art,
We find the beauty of the heart.

Chronicles of Unanswered Prayers

Kneeling on a cold stone floor,
Whispers rise in longing air.
Echoes of hope in shadows soar,
Yet silence answers me in despair.

Blessed hands reach to the sky,
Yet doubts invade the gentle sigh.
Promises linger, spirits fly,
In the stillness, my heart asks why.

Tears like rain on barren ground,
I cry for grace, but none is found.
Faith feels lost, no solace around,
In this struggle, weariness is crowned.

Clouds of doubt obscure the light,
I search for solace in the night.
Mountains vast stand out of sight,
While my prayers drift like a kite.

Yet still I stand, hands open wide,
In the void, my spirit bides.
From these ashes, I won't hide,
For hope endures where faith abides.

The Holy Dusk of Us

In twilight's glow, we find our grace,
Hearts entwined in sacred space.
Under the veil where shadows trace,
We whisper dreams, a holy embrace.

Your eyes, a mirror, show the way,
As evening stars begin to play.
In stillness deep, our spirits sway,
In love's soft hush, we choose to stay.

Every prayer in silence speaks,
A promise bound, to love it seeks.
Though the world may challenge weeks,
In our hearts, faith never leaks.

The dusk unfolds, a canvas wide,
We walk together, side by side.
In the whispers where dreams reside,
Our souls unite, in love, we bide.

Though storms may rise and shadows loom,
In the sacred dusk, love finds room.
Through every trial, our hearts bloom,
In faith we dance, dispelling gloom.

Fragile Faith in a Withered Garden

Among the weeds, my faith does grow,
In soil cracked, where sorrows flow.
Petals fall like tears of woe,
Yet hope still whispers soft and low.

Roots dig deep through darkened earth,
Searching for signs of life and birth.
In fragile blooms, I find my worth,
Through trials faced, I hold my mirth.

Sunlight breaks the clouds so gray,
As shadows dance and fears decay.
In this garden where spirits play,
I nurture dreams, come what may.

Every bud, a prayer in bloom,
Defiant against despair's looming gloom.
In whispers soft, I find my room,
A sanctuary where love can groom.

And though the seasons may change the scene,
I'll trust the growth, though it seems lean.
From barren ground, my soul will glean,
In faith, I cherish what's unseen.

Divine Solitude Amongst the Ruins

Amidst the rubble, silence reigns,
In solitude, my spirit gains.
Whispers of angels, gentle strains,
In the wreckage, love remains.

Each broken stone tells tales of grace,
Where once was joy, now time lays waste.
But in these ruins, I embrace,
The sacred whispers, the heart's soft pace.

With each breath, I find my ground,
In the echoes, a truth profound.
God's light in shadows can be found,
A solace in the lost, unbound.

In stillness clear, I raise my eyes,
To the heavens where hope lies.
Through endless night, beneath starry skies,
My heart awakens, begins to rise.

In solitude, I feel the call,
Amidst the ruins, I'm not small.
For in these moments, I stand tall,
Divine presence holds us all.

The Veil of Unsaid Goodbyes

In silence we part, in shadows we dwell,
Words left unspoken, a lingering spell.
Hearts aching softly, like petals that fall,
A moment of truth within love's quiet call.

The weight of the silence, a bittersweet grace,
As tears trace the path of this hallowed space.
With faith as our guide, we traverse the unknown,
Trusting in whispers that carry us home.

The light dims around us, yet hope finds a way,
In the hush of our parting, we silently pray.
For love never fades, though we may not perceive,
The bonds that unite us, the ties that believe.

So take with you pieces of all we have shared,
Embrace the unknown, know my heart's always bared.
Though distance may linger, our spirits align,
In the cosmos of souls, our light will still shine.

Ethereal Whispers of Departure

As dawn breaks the night, soft whispers arise,
In the hush of the morning, where solace lies.
Echoes of longing trace curves of the heart,
With grace in their steps, we prepare to depart.

Each moment a prayer, each breath a sweet sigh,
With love boundless and wide, we reach for the sky.
In shadows and light, the spirits entwine,
A tender reminder of what is divine.

Resilient we stand, though parting feels raw,
The tapestry woven reveals the great law.
In every goodbye, there's a blessing concealed,
An eternal embrace where our fates are revealed.

With faith as our anchor, we drift on the breeze,
Carried by whispers from trees and from seas.
The beauty of endings births beginnings anew,
In the realm of the heart, I will always find you.

The Confessional of My Solitude

In the stillness of night, my soul bares its truth,
Before unseen angels, reclaiming my youth.
Each secret laid bare, a confession to space,
In the silence, I seek my lost sacred place.

A heart wrapped in shadows, yet seeking the light,
Through whispers of prayer that banish the fright.
In solitude's arms, I gather my thoughts,
A sanctuary built from the battles I fought.

With every regret, a lesson bestowed,
The weight of the past, like a heavy-load road.
Yet in this confessional, hope's ember gleams,
Awakening visions from deep, restless dreams.

To the heavens I call, to the stars I confide,
In the arms of my solace, I open wide.
For wisdom borne of silence speaks volumes so loud,
As I stand in my truth, unashamed and proud.

Vestiges of Love's Sacrifice

In the echoes of time, love's legacy lingers,
Carved in the silence, etched deep with fingers.
For every sacrifice, a story remains,
In shadows of longing, love's essence regains.

With hearts intertwined, we traverse the divine,
In moments of pain, the light starts to shine.
Each tear that we shed waters gardens of grace,
In the tapestry woven, we find our place.

Through trials we walk, hand in hand, side by side,
In the furnace of love, our spirits abide.
For what we let go, a new bloom will rise,
In the echoes of sacrifice, love never dies.

The vestiges linger, like whispers in dreams,
In the depths of the heart, light endlessly beams.
Together we stand, strong in our plight,
For love is the spark that ignites the night.

Pilgrimage Through Wounded Memories

In shadows deep where sorrows dwell,
Each step I take, a tolling bell.
Through winding paths of love and loss,
I bear the weight, I carry the cross.

With weary eyes, I seek the light,
In every dark, there flickers bright.
The echoes of a distant grace,
Remind me of my rightful place.

Each heartfelt prayer, a whisper soft,
Rising high as I lift aloft.
For wounds may heal, but still they ache,
In silent night, for peace I wake.

The journey calls through trials and pain,
In every loss, there's much to gain.
A testament of faith renewed,
My spirit soars, and love is true.

Upon the stones, my footprints lay,
In every step, I find my way.
For hope reborn in shadows deep,
A sacred promise I shall keep.

Beneath the Cross of Silent Regret

In twilight's hush, where shadows loom,
I seek the light to pierce the gloom.
Each tear that falls, a prayer unsaid,
Beneath the cross, my heart has bled.

Through whispered dreams and fading sighs,
I search for truth, in starlit skies.
Regrets like thorns, they pierce my soul,
Yet mercy's hand can make me whole.

I kneel in silence, broken yet bold,
Among the ashes of stories told.
Each moment lost, a lesson learned,
In shadows dark, my spirit burned.

Forgiveness waits, a gentle breeze,
A balm for wounds, my heart's disease.
I rise again, though burdened still,
For strength abounds within God's will.

Beneath the weight, I find my peace,
In every prayer, my soul's release.
The cross I bear, though heavy, pure,
Leads me to hope, forever sure.

Sacrament of the Unspoken

In quietude, the heart's refrain,
Speaks volumes of our sacred pain.
Each silence holds a truth divine,
In whispered prayers, our souls entwine.

The sacred act of holding tight,
To love concealed in darkest night.
In mirrored eyes, reflections glide,
A language felt, no words to bide.

The sacrament of what we share,
Transcends the burden, lifts the care.
Through every glance, a promise keeps,
In gentle sighs, the spirit leaps.

Our hearts, a vessel of the meek,
In solitude, we fast and seek.
Each unspoken word a beacon bright,
Guiding us home through endless night.

In seraphim's embrace we find,
The solace offered by the Kind.
Eternal love, a dance of hope,
In silence held, our souls elope.

Transgressions of the Heart's Sanctuary

In hallowed halls where shadows sigh,
The heart exposed, a solemn cry.
Transgressions haunt with each lost beat,
Yet grace pours forth, a healing sweet.

With trembling hands, I search for light,
To mend the cracks and set things right.
Each whisper shared, a balm for pain,
In seeking love, I hope to gain.

The sacred space within my soul,
Awaits redemption, makes me whole.
A fragile heart, but fierce in trust,
In mercy's grace, I rise from dust.

Forgive the wounds, the scars remain,
In every loss, a glimpse of gain.
Transgressions teach the soul to yearn,
For love's embrace, in tides we turn.

In reverence, I bow and pray,
For strength to rise, for light to stay.
The sanctuary holds my fears,
In sacred silence, I shed tears.

Milton Keynes UK
Ingram Content Group UK Ltd.
UKHW021836301124
451618UK00007BA/176

9 789916 898116